wisequacks

A Renaissance book

First published in 2006 by New Holland Publishers (NZ) Ltd
Auckland • Sydney • London • Cape Town

218 Lake Road, Northcote, Auckland, New Zealand
14 Aquatic Drive, Frenchs Forest, NSW 2086, Australia
86-88 Edgware Road, London, W2 2EA, United Kingdom
80 McKenzie Street, Cape Town 8001, South Africa

www.newhollandpublishers.co.nz

Copyright © 2006 in photography: Ian Baker
Copyright © 2006 New Holland Publishers (NZ) Ltd

ISBN–13: 978 1 86966 122 9
ISBN–10: 1 86966 122 2

Packaged for New Holland Publishers in
2006 by Renaissance Publishing, Auckland
Design: Trevor Newman

A catalogue record for this book is available
from the National Library of New Zealand

10 9 8 7 6 5 4 3 2 1

Colour reproduction by
SC (Sang Choy) International Pte Ltd,
Singapore
Printed in China through
Phoenix Offset, Hong Kong

wise quacks

photography by IAN BAKER

NEW HOLLAND

There is probably nothing like living together for blinding people to each other.

Ivy Compton-Burnett

**I give myself sometimes
admirable advice, but
I am incapable of taking it.**

Lady Mary Wortley Montagu

It is amazing how much can be accomplished if no one cares who gets the credit.

John Wooden

I like long walks, especially when they

are taken by people who annoy me. Noel Coward

**There were times when
it seemed to him that the
different parts of him were not
all under the same management.**

Russell Hoban

Sleep is when all the unsorted stuff comes flying out as from a dustbin upset in a high wind.

William Golding

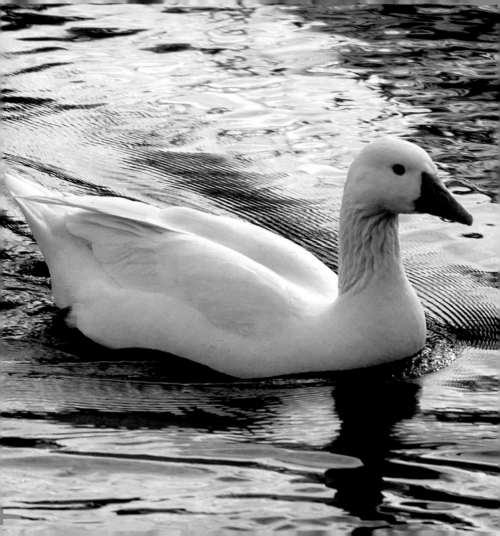

There are few who would not rather be taken in adultery than in provincialism.

Aldous Huxley

Life is a foreign language: all men mispronounce it.

Christopher Morley

**Advice is like kissing:
It costs nothing and it's a
pleasant thing to do.**

George Bernard Shaw

Infinity is a dreadfully poor place. They can never manage to make ends meet.

Norton Juster

Learn from the mistakes of others. You can't live long enough to make them all yourself.

Eleanor Roosevelt

Nothing so conclusively proves a man's ability to lead others as what he does from day to day to lead himself.

Thomas J. Watson

The trouble with political jokes is that very often they get elected!

Will Rogers

**I never read a book
before reviewing it;
it prejudices a man so.**

Sydney Smith

**Don't do anything
you wouldn't be willing to
explain on television.**

Arjay Miller

It is unbecoming for young men to utter maxims.

Aristotle

You know more than you think you do.

Dr Benjamin Spock

Meetings are rather like cocktail parties. You don't want to go, but you're cross not to be asked.

Jilly Cooper

The trouble with jogging is that by the time you realize you're not in shape for it, it's too far to walk back.

Franklin Jones

**Father, Mother and me,
Sister and Auntie say
All the people like us are We
And everyone else is They.**

Rudyard Kipling

Idleness is impossible to enjoy thoroughly

unless one has plenty of work to do. Jerome K. Jerome

I do not believe that friends
are necessarily the people
you like best, they are
merely the people who got
there first.

Peter Ustinov

So live that you wouldn't be ashamed to sell the family parrot to the town gossip.

Will Rogers

Camping is nature's way of promoting the motel business.

Dave Barry

Politicians are the same all over. They promise to build a bridge even where there's no river.

Nikita S. Khrushchev

Gnaw not thy nails in the presence of others, nor bite them with thy teeth.

Francis Hawkins

**Let's get out of these
wet clothes and
into a dry martini.**

Mae West

There's nothing like eavesdropping to show you that the world outside your head is different from the world inside your head.

Thornton Wilder

Alcohol is a very necessary article ... it enables Parliament to do things at eleven at night that no sane person would do at eleven in the morning.

George Bernard Shaw

Courtship is that period of time during which the female decides whether or not she can do any better.

E.C. McKenzie

I believe in loyalty.
When a woman reaches
an age she likes,
she should stick with it.

Eva Gabor

Education is an admirable thing, but it is well to remember from time to time that nothing worth knowing can be taught.

Oscar Wilde

Insanity is a perfectly rational adjustment to an insane world.

R.D. Laing

Where two or three are gathered together, that is about enough.

Les A. Murray

A 'good family', it seems,

is one that used to be better. Cleveland Amory

Children are nature's own form of birth control.

Dave Barry

**Always do right;
this will gratify some people
and astonish the rest.**

Mark Twain

You can't drown yourself in drink. I've tried, you float.

John Barrymore

If this raised a laugh, then try these
other Farmyard Wisdom titles:

Bray for Inspiration
Chewing the Cud
Fowl Play
Pig Tales
Woolly Wisdom